Underdog Psychosis

How deprived socio-economic conditions and lack of
stimulation can cause underdog psychosis

Stephen Connell

DEDICATION

This book is dedicated to Naya Isabel Connell

CONTENTS

ACKNOWLEDGMENTS

We learn from our mistakes, I thank all the situations and confrontations that caused me to write this book. In addition I thank my close friends and family for helping me form an opinion... Free Santz

A special thank you to Agnes S. Dunsire Langeland; you are a star.

Chapter 1 Underdog psychosis

"Underdog psychosis spreading around in the hood like flu.
The security guard follows me around like I haven't got £2 to pay for my
juice."-Skepta[i]

Every motion, every thought, every lesson learnt contributes to the person you are currently. However, only recently have I come to terms with the idea that not only do we shape our own personalities but the environment we are in and what is around us, shapes us even more.

Underdog psychosis is a phrase coined by a London artist called Skepta. In an online video he explains how the educational system failed him personally, sending his high school and teen years on a tangent of what is known as the socially accepted path. As a young black teenager, going through high school is a world of distractions and choices, choices that could potentially change the outcome of your life. Personally I have seen peers, including myself, take this for granted. We skipped class, we smoked weed from an early age, we chased girls, we had fights and "we did road more than school." We sat in class and said:

1

"Fuck this; fuck Pythagoras"

These are understandable thoughts when you've already convinced you yourself will not achieve. Understandable thoughts when any career you may have will not involve anything as complicated as what you're currently learning. Why is that? Why are our thoughts this way? Why did we skip class? Why did we smoke and sell weed from a young age? Why are our assumptions correct? Why don't we succeed?

"The cave you fear to enter holds the treasure you seek."-Joseph Campbell[ii]

What is underdog psychosis?

Here are the dictionary definitions;

Underdog

Noun.

1. A person who is expected to lose in a contester conflict.

2. A victim of social or political injustice

Psychosis

noun

1.   A mental disorder characterised by symptoms, such as delusions or hallucinations that indicate impaired contact with reality.

My interpretation may be different to those reading, however, what I personally gathered from the phrase is that we are destined to be underdogs; we are moulded to accept society as it is. We have been masked and brainwashed, taking away our view of reality. How?

I propose the fact that there may be two different types of underdog psychosis based on our sink or swim mechanisms. Some of us who are affected by underdog psychosis either accept our socio-economic circumstance or strive to change it. Those who strive to change it, statistically do so in vain.

Adopting a false reality, we believe we are in control of our thoughts and dreams but instead fail to realise that by the time we have decided to play we have already lost.

If life is a game, then we are the players.

Who are we playing against?

Life is full of smoke and mirrors we believe we are playing against each other but the truth is we are all playing against the system *literally.* Politics, (*clearly labelled as it may be*) is also very much a game of smoke and mirrors. It is obviously difficult to attend to the desires and needs of everybody in a group and even more challenging to resolve conflicts of interest within groups whilst also attending to your own desires and needs. There is no right, there is no wrong, and they are chosen by the masses and given the power.

Right and wrong are chosen by the higher powers and imposed on the masses. If you are a minority and working class, then you have no choice. You do not decide. Is it right to kill one to save ten? Is it right to squash a minority to boost a majority? Honestly, I understand that without destitution we are without riches, however, why are we forced to stay on one side? Why do we even allow this?

The choice of who you become may be stripped from you as a child. As black people from socially deprived areas, we have no role models. Every character in every story book read to us as children, every main character on every cartoon or TV show reinforces the fact that good is portrayed as lighter skinned and rich, and bad is poor and darker skinned. Even to the effect that the black-based characters in most cartoons are stereotypically portrayed as lazy, procrastinating low lives. In particular, I would like to highlight Jim Crow, from the Disney cartoon Dumbo, who is portrayed as a jazz singing crow that loiters and smokes outside with his friends all day and is notoriously lazy. Even worse is that 'the crows' speak in a way that's stereotypical of old black men. Furthermore, in a pilot episode of the Simpsons, which is rare to see on TV, the original Smithers character (the servant to the richest man in town) was black.

This idea is mirrored in a phrase coined by Spike Lee known as the "magical negro". At a lecture in Washington he explained that the Hollywood film industry introduced the magical negro, a black character with magical powers that helps the main character (who in most cases is white). He then proclaims that Morgan Freeman is the biggest example. He is right. In "Bruce Almighty" he is just trying to help poor underdog Bruce. In *The Dark Knight Trilogy* he helps Batman enhance and enable his superpower of white-privilege... and lets not get into *The Shawshank Redemption*

This idea of a magical negro can also be seen in *The Matrix*. Secretly I am a fan of *The Matrix*, however, I'm not going to point out the obvious character Morpheus because he was not magical as he had the same powers as Neo. In fact do you remember the character the Oracle? Yes, the only character that can help Neo with magic advice, he/she is the real magical negro.

Another example is *Safe House* with Denzel Washington. Despite being a protagonist in the movie he is also the older, wiser black man who gives the rookie white character advice. South Park tried to address this issue by ironically adding a character called Token; the only black kid in the town. Despite this, they still have a large, smooth jazz singing chef that gives the kids advice in most episodes. From my perspective this is a form of modern day institutionalised racism; almost as if black people are being thrown a bone to disguise the fact we still have no power. We are still not in control.

The world is against you underdog; so keep your head up.

In all stages of our younger years we are susceptible to the world. This is when our mind is young and new; the perfect time to be moulded. Instead of the poor environment moulding our youth, WE need to mould our youth ourselves. Very slowly, there have been small changes that are breaking through the dirt like new seedlings. I see more people screaming for a change but with no logical answer. "Stop racism!" This is a great idea, with great meaning behind it, but how can you alter a mind-set? How can you stop something that has been a staple of your environment since your youth? We need to educate our youth to understand the challenges they will face till it is no more. Knowledge will change everything. Knowledge is power.

How do you hide information from black people?

Put it in a book.

Jokes and techniques used during slavery. How do you take the power away from potentially powerful people? Take away their intelligence and knowledge. Beat them till all they see is pain and can't fight anymore. Our generation was taught by a generation that *got used to* systemic racism, once blatant racism was made ultimately taboo. Our parents' generation had to deal with the glass ceiling. Being told you have no limits, until you hit that barrier and imaginary sign reading "no black man or woman shall pass!" Feeding you the dream that with enough work and effort you can keep on climbing. Thus, we were taught that higher education and schooling is the only way. In addition to the fact that there are no positive role models in the media, we are lead to believe that without a university education we are worthless and deemed unskilled in the game.

Underdog psychosis spreading around in the hood like flu.
The security guard follows me around like I haven't got £2 to pay for my juice
Now all this bullshit got me smoking this stupid zoot
Tell Boris he's lucky I made it rapping I would have been looting too
Skepta[iii]

Honestly, if you felt you had nothing and were constantly fed the ideology that you need to have more, whilst a riot is happening and you were an opportunist like some of those in the London riots. Wouldn't you go out there and get a large TV you know you are never going to be able to buy? Wouldn't you get some fresh clothes and before running to the next shop, stop off at mc Donald's where someone's turned on the cooker and is frying burgers? Riots were caused by the unjust actions of the police.

Wouldn't you take an opportunity to say, "Fuck you" and throw a bottle at a police officer, grab free burgers, clothes and electrical goods? I would. This is what's so crucial; observe the power we have when we have one objective. We also need to teach the younger generations how to elevate themselves into positions of power.

We are our own worst enemy. I remember when I felt that my childhood dream of becoming a pilot disappeared. I remember I found myself on a small pilot course to give me a taster of pilot life. Through the RAF I met a boy called Toby. Firstly, Toby's family were extremely rich, he also had a couple of 100 more hours of flight time than I did. Each hour of flight time cost a few hundred pounds, not including fuel and Toby explained to me that the path to becoming a pilot is expensive. If you're not a straight A student there's no chance of a full scholarship and even if you get a licence, to get a job you basically have to be the nephew of Mr. Branson. All I could think was, "if he is finding it hard, I'm pissed!"

This was difficult to digest and so, weakened by lack of knowledge, I chose the easy way out. We all do. I have spent money I shouldn't have.

I have mistreated my peers. I have put down others for my personal gain. I drink, I smoke and I chose not to educate myself. I have been my own worst enemy.

I left high school with better grades then most of the people I saw day to day. However, eager to join the forever-losing game of life and thinking that university almost seemed impossible, my drive and push slowly vanished. Looking back, the work was not that difficult, the effort was not tremendous. It was just me. I did not push myself, including the fact I knew I was never going to make it as a pilot. To be truthful I did try, although not for my own benefit but because I was told it was the best option for me. However, once settled in, I did not apply myself nor did I take college seriously. With my dying passion at the time, also died my chances of a somewhat stable lifestyle. We are our own worst enemies; we see those with more than us and feel confused as to why we do not have the same. Wouldn't you want to even the playing field? Wouldn't you feel forced into a corner thus choosing crime as a career choice? I mean, let's be honest. Most of the role models in my life were only well off due to crime. What am I to turn to?

This mentality is dangerous and keeps us below the glass ceiling; we have been forced to think this way. Forced to crime, through lack of education and stimulation, through lack of aspirations and dreams. Our effort and power is put into so many things we could do without. Trapped in the cycle where not many prosper, how do you elevate yourself? We think very individually, but to rise up, elevate ourselves and succeed as a team we need to change our starting point. We need to elevate everyone around us; we need to give ourselves a new norm so that when an individual rises he or she is not set back before they even get a chance.

We separate ourselves into further groups and then squabble amongst each other over trivial situations. Fighting amongst each other only takes away our power as a group. A slave owner named Willie Lynch[iv], fathomed a theory about how to divide the black race during slavery. For the latter to be accomplished, Lynch noted that because of the unstable history and treatment, most slaves have a mild hatred of each other; this hatred is what Lynch capitalised from.

"Let us make a slave. What do we need? First of all, we need a black nigger man, a pregnant nigger woman and her baby nigger boy. Second, we will use the same basic principle that we use in breaking a horse, combined with some more sustaining factors. What we do with horses is that we break them from one form of life to another; that is, we reduce them from their natural state in nature. Whereas nature provides them with the natural capacity to take care of their offspring, we break that natural string of independence from them and thereby create a dependency status, so that we may be able to get from them useful production for our business and pleasure." – Willie lynch- Letter 1712

Lynch was a plantation owner in the Caribbean in the 1700s, but these words still echo in modern day life. Make them love their masters and destroy each other Lynch writes a whole thesis on how to control a slave; he basically writes that the black race will forever be subservient because it has been drilled into us. However, what if he is correct? It is the same modern day theory, by destroying our history and ambitions we are left without direction. Left only to believe that we are wrong and they are right.

We are wrong and they are right.

Delete the mind set when you feel you may never make it. University isn't for everyone. Delete the bad energy that makes you consider crime as an acceptable path. Delete the attitude and contribute to raising your community. You can be what to want to be. Kindly I urge you young adults in school to challenge yourself; school systems are not going to help you if you don't try to help yourselves.

Try brand new things for no reason. Experience life other places than in your usual surroundings. Evolve. If you are a product of your environment, expand your environment. Expand your knowledge of other cultures, expand your knowledge of your history, and expand on learning how powerful you are.

Try following Skepta's philosophy of life:

Too much TV, too many newspapers got a nigga thinking evil
Got me thinking I'm looking at my enemy when I'm looking at my own people
Notice when a white man looks at my watch I think he's trying to pay me a compliment
When a black man looks at my watch I think he's trying to knock my confidence (mad)
I was in Amsterdam smoking blue cheese and I had an epiphany

All these negative preconceptions just bring more negativity

Instead of investing in new businesses they buy new artillery

Everybody in the hood wants to spray a 16 and I don't mean lyrically [v]

I confess to not having written a book before. This is because I had no interest. No desires to want to do anything other than attempt to get rich by any route. I have travelled far for large ventures and I've been running around with smaller ventures. However my biggest venture is yet to come.

As I'm writing this, my girlfriend and I are having a baby girl. As I lay up next to my girlfriend, I think about this little child coming into this life and I am scared. Scared that this world has so many flaws. Scared that I need to teach this girl how to shield herself from the effects of these flaws. Otherwise who knows what could happen? So I have written this book to give my child and other children a book that doesn't automatically assume you to be wrong, to give them a foundation. I have written this book at several stages at a time in my life when things are very **fast** paced. Please understand these opinions expressed are my personal thoughts, and any readers who take offence must understand these are my thoughts and not those of every ethnic or "urban" person living in London.

I digress. A friend I see once in a while said something to me earlier that made me smile but at the exact same time sent my mood on a slight decline. After discussing his confusion as to why plain clothes police officers are constantly looking at his moped as if they are looking to find something wrong to put against him. He said, "Fuck them. When I had a bike I used that bike to buy me a car... The bastards took that... But then I got on my grind and legit got a bike and now they are trying to find something wrong. Well fuck them because the bike is going to buy me a car and then that car will get me the R8". I love to know he wants a r8 and is aspiring towards wealth and success however it is crazy to know that he's 18 and knows how difficult it will be for him because he is black growing up in Church Road, Harlesden.

"The chief patient I am preoccupied with is myself" - Sigmund Freud [vi]

Chapter 2 Ideas

"More time I'm tryna show man the vision
But it's like man are still too poor to see
So I let man do their ting
I ain't judging anybody, I don't wanna law degree" –Skepta [vii]

A philosopher called Hegel [viii]wrote several books, which are very long and difficult to understand. However, once you grasp what he is trying to say the message becomes very modern. Hegel lived at a time where people looked at past ideas and views as inferior: Sound familiar? He says as a society we look back to our predecessors' ideas and plans as if they are immediately wrong. Hegel urged people of his time to look at previous philosophers and artists, for ideas they may have overlooked or cast out. Every era has a depository of information that we can choose to learn from. What will future philosophers and historians learn about us? We frequently discard ideas from people we look to be socially or economically beneath us. In reality we should be accepting ideas from socially or economically inferior groups to incite a decisive change rather than a destructive change.

Progress is not linear. We need to learn from ideas that we may dislike at first. The idea of a solemn community can be taken from ancient Greece; even with their ancient flaws. Furthermore, the idea of honor can be mostly seen during the Middle Ages; ideas which contribute from the past that make a tolerable world to live in. However, leaving history aside and looking more towards the communities and societies we deem as a different class or as inferior, we find solidarity. For example, the somewhat noble solidarity at times of hardship can be seen naturally in socially and economically deprived groups. You could almost call it social patriotism. This contributes to making life in modern London very tolerable. I suggest that the ideology taken away from my culture could be the idea of entrepreneurialism. Selim Bassoul CEO of the Middleby Corporation "The biggest reason people become an entrepreneur is self-doubt and conflict, now if you have nothing to lose then you become an entrepreneur." [ix] Those with the disposition of underdog psychosis have nothing to lose, giving them natural abilities to become entrepreneurs. It makes sense; our "hustle" culture derives from social and economic deprivation. This culture revolves around a very simple story of the underdog. It is what is marketed for the masses to buy into.

Grime is an expression of our culture. It is our art.

Grime is one of the largest platforms for our culture and an avid listener to UK rap and grime would know that most of it is about the underdog and the expression of feelings and stories that their audiences relates to.

During Hegel's era, art was used to control the masses through the idea of religion. Art basically portrayed the ideologies that historians and philosophers wanted society to have. Therefore art played a huge role in history, not only leaving us almost cryptic meanings to decipher through images and sculptures, but to help govern and direct the society of the time. I feel we are in the internet/digital era, where much of the information or contacts you need are accessible via your computer. Art, although similar to how it used to be, is no longer used to inspire or govern the masses. Instead, it has become a source of expression. Some would argue that the idea of expression is the new message we need to impose on everyone. However, I believe that the power of being able to induce ideas and govern has fallen to audio and visual art. In my opinion Hegel would be urging us to use any platform we have to spread our ideologies to each other. This is how we can help our **own** culture to develop and grow. We already have platforms we use and watch that are controlled by us. We need to use these platforms and spread the understanding of building and educating our culture. We have built our own smaller society; the people who are at the forefront should be pushing for the idea of empowerment and change. If every artist were to rap and sing about elevation of the mind paired with trap-like motivation music, we would have a solid message to give to our youth that isn't watered down.

"Art is the sensuous presentation of ideas." [x]

Hegel speaks a lot about founding new institutions. The world we currently live in is a world of institutions and corporations. Large companies and institutions have the power money and time to do large-scale projects that those smaller institutions cannot. My point is even this book will need help from an external institution to reach the heights and limits that I will not be able to create in a small amount of time. However, we are not to dismiss our predecessors' efforts, but rather we should exploit them to incite change. Therefore, the right kinds of institution are crucial in order for us to progress.

Mistakes

"Do you regret any of your decisions?" A question asked to me by a friend. Without digressing into a past of poor decisions and choices, my answer is no. Simply because all of the mistakes and resulting lessons I learnt, contribute to what makes me, me. Everybody makes mistakes. Everyone will lose himself or herself from time to time. It is what makes us human.

"I think therefore I am."- Descartes [xi]

We are all affected by what we see and read. Personality is a sign of us being conscious, conscious of our surroundings and our environment. The fact that everybody has considerably distinctive personalities proves that everybody is also conscious and thinking.

Mistakes are often looked at as terrible things we cringe to think about. However, we should look to our mistakes for guidance on future decisions. Our personality and confidence are directly related to the mistakes made or lack of mistakes made in our lives. Therefore we are not to look at the mistakes we may have made personally or the mistakes our predecessors made, but we are to learn from them. Through adversity and hardship we have to succeed. We cannot lose this game.

Have you ever sold drugs? Hopefully you can read and safely say no. Which is great! but let's pretend you sell drugs. Do you know how much motivation it takes to actually go out there to sell drugs on the road? It takes an immense amount of energy and effort to walk around the high road all day gathering numbers of people who look like they could potentially take drugs. Then to later do some market messaging to all your new clientele?

Diddy speaks in an interview about the hustler's spirit. I believe Diddy is trying to give a phrase to the almost psychopathic drive that pushes someone from a disadvantaged background to become an entrepreneur. I believe that this is natural for some people who have been living in a less sheltered environment from an early age, and some people develop a hunger for it after they have landed in a conflict situation. The drive that gets you up to keep going to the point where you have worked so hard even when you have achieved your goals you still cannot stop working. This is the key attribute that I can see may be gained from living on the disadvantaged team. This is what we need to spread and share amongst us.

Red pill or blue pill?

We are not the only ones who are fed the lie about life choices. The idea that everybody, equally and with the same amount of effort and knowledge, can reach the heights in their personal and professional life. We are misguided if we believe that we have the same chances and make similar choices. Alternatively, they are equally misguided in a mild, blind white prejudice to think that there is not a problem. The difference is the understanding of this concept and to be mindful. Just do you. Just do what you need to do to build yourself, your family and then those around you. That is all you need to do.

Everybody has a hustler's spirit. However I feel it may take a few life-changing moments to really bring it out in you, moments that people in socio-economically deprived groups may encounter more often than other middle-class groups. This constant pressure is cooking your hustler's spirit till you feel it is time to make a change. Naturally we turn to money because we live in a western capitalist society that shows you that the only way up is with more money.

Most of the role models we see are well off because of crime. Therefore it is natural to think the only way up is through crime. We need to rub out comments the unconfident phrases we speak to our kids with;

"People like us don't..."or "know your place...". Rub that mentality out. For the next generation to prosper we need to all think positively. We need to think of our culture and community as a big company we all own; all putting our separate part into it. Obviously the aim is to take the initiative and become the best you can be. However, by being the best you can, you will also help the area you live in to become better. We have to help each other by helping ourselves.

"I had teachers who doubted me,

Told me I wouldn't make it

This time next year in the playground

I'm gonna park up my spaceship"-Yxng Bane[xii]

My mum, dad and brother have moved to Atlanta to start their new lives in America. They tell me it is a state with a black government where they have built their own community and corporations. This gave me two positive viewpoints. Firstly the idea of a self-serving, self-sustainable government even though there are racial issues, they have a black government. Secondly my father spoke of an appreciation of being able to drive a nice car without it seeming abnormal because of his skin colour.

Imagine that happening in London and other places with socio-economic deprivation. Imagine a society that had a multicultural understanding. A government that understands the concept of perpetuating growth and social mobility. Imagine living somewhere with a universal understanding of change, with the ability to adapt in a democratic way.

Plato[xiii] sometimes used to write some lessons and teachings in the form of analogies so his audience could understand. One story is about the three men chained in a cave. Three men are chained in a cave; they can only see shadows on the wall cast by the outside world. The have been chained in the cave since birth and therefore the cave and these shadows are all they know. The three men are able to put words to shapes cast on the walls by shadows and the sounds they heard as things moved past the outside of the cave. One day one man is freed. In a burst of interest he ventures outside where he learns that the shadows they used to see were actually cast by physical objects and the sun. Not until the man sees his own reflection in a lake, does he rush back to the cave. The freed man runs to explain what he has seen and tries to free the other two. The two chained men violently resist, claiming that the change of being freed has made him crazy and delusional. Plato says this is what it is like to be a philosopher in his time, trying to tell society (the chained men) about a new concept or understanding.

Being complacent is one of my biggest fears. It's probably subconsciously the reason I wrote this book. Human beings may become comfortable, too comfortable even. I hear conversations of having to accept the way the world is and just accept that it is rubbish. These people are the chained men in the story. Enduring their current situation and not pushing for changes. However, the freed man challenged himself to know more and go somewhere he had never been before. Do not be the chained men, comfortable with the knowledge and level you are currently at. Those who endure life with this underdog psychosis do not believe they can be authors of change and understanding.

Are the masses too stubborn and ignorant to govern themselves? Yes. Sadly true. What I write is an ideology, a thesis that has understanding but takes a lot to be put into practice. We need people to light the flame. We need people who want to change their lives first so they can change the lives of others. This is not a 5-year plan, ladies and gentlemen.

For there to be natural progression of the world we need to have an ever-changing environment so as to incite change and to bring through new powers that can incorporate new ideas. So hypothetically speaking, if we had our own publishing agent publishing books from authors from our culture, we could make a definite stamp on history. With our current institutions this almost seems impossible. Basically, for an idea to be active and effective, it needs a lot more than just to be correct. For example, I try to share my ideas so they help everyone equally rather than one culture or section of society; in my eyes my ideas are "correct" but they will not be powerful or effective without the correct backing and institutions. New institutions will help us develop change. Only through education of ourselves and our descendants will we incite change.

Chapter 3   Power

"People are profoundly illiterate in power"- Eric Liu[xiv]

Eric Liu, who is a writer and founder of Citizen University, states that ordinary people do not understand power: neither how power is created nor how it affects you. I believe this stems all the way down into societies and communities. Although we understand we have a power that may be higher than us, we have no knowledge about how it was formed or how a specific group of people with power affects us. Basically, as my previous chapters suggest, we have too little power and control. How can we want to be seen as equal if equality isn't generally thought possible? Of course we have no prominent voice in the conversation of those who rule our country because we do not own our own foundations or networks that have been self-sustainable. My argument is before we can push for equality; we would need an equal leg to stand on. Without meaning to sound repetitive but this could be achieved by spreading the understanding of power and progression.

Chimamanda Ngozi Adichie, who is a globally recognised author, says in a speech that she was an early learner. She was rumoured to learn how to read at the age of two and says she used to write stories as a child in Nigeria. She found it hilarious when she reflected on the fact that all of her characters she wrote about where white, and loved to talk about the weather. It is crazy how someone so far from western culture can be affected so dramatically by the one-sided argument. She felt that there were too few stories dealing with black people.

The influence of a privileged white culture is so strong it had affected her life as a child; I don't remember including many black characters into stories I wrote as a child. It's as if we do not see ourselves as any part of this culture from a young age. You are shown the power divide in our cultures even from a privileged white point of view. It is unreasonable to deny the clear social feeling of divide and rule, and where power lies. We are born into a world that is essentially westernised, underlining white status. A considerable amount of children's books show scenarios and settings that portray black and coloured peoples exclusion from the general culture. In fact, black characters with both power and influence are hugely underrepresented in literature.

Socially, we view things that have longstanding strength and command to be power factors, which is a questionable concept. We will have no real power, not until we build and have control over our own assets; which is not a five-year plan. I am a part of a new culture one never seen before. The inner city London boy, the loud, grime music generation. However our budding culture that naturally blossomed from the **divide** can mark the birth of real power. It is the beginning of having control over something that is unmistakably ours.

I walked past Harrods and they had a window display, which left me confused. The manikins wore cuffed tracksuit trousers, "Air max" type trainers, a bomber jacket and a baseball cap. The manikins might as well have had 8ths in their pockets. They were basically selling our fashion style. Harrods had our culture on display, and were making money off essentially something we all had part in creating. This is why we need power. We are exploited and never receive a penny; this has been happening longer than I have been alive. Now is the dawn where we should get in on this and make money from our attributes. We need to start owning and changing parts of our city. We need to look at what we want the future to be and what we have to do to change it.

We can have power in all sectors. Music and fashion are examples because they are universal and easily researched; Grime and UK Rap is an example of this new power. In my lifetime I have witnessed and been a part of the birth and growth of this influential genre. A sound that comes from a social viewpoint; this music expresses social understanding, that a lot of people are in the same boat. With this music we are beginning to see people from our culture taking command. Having their words reach millions, added to the fact that these people are actually listening: that's power!

Some readers will know people who are "career criminals"; some who have a network of workers and a chain of supply and a chain of demand from drugs, stolen goods, fraud etc. Oddly enough even though crime is their career they had easily accomplished the basics of most conglomerate companies, merged smaller endeavours to a larger movement. Attacked and submerged competition, even branching into other fields not necessarily the same as their prior. This is done usually without major guidance... I mean there aren't many books on how to do road 2016. Life is filled with too many variables for there to be a specific way. With this in mind, a group of people, who are deemed incapable and worthless, were able to accumulate wealth from their natural ability to build even with the odds of life against them. Imagine this power aimed in the right direction. Imagine the drugs were swapped for a legitimate home-grown product in demand. The attitude would certainly change. Obviously this doesn't happen overnight. The idea of everybody putting down drugs and guns and swapping them for high paid jobs with bonuses is as stupid as screaming "stop racism" and expecting everybody to stop. However all we can do is take our current situation and use the emerging powers we have to create progress in our smaller communities so they in turn push larger communities to want to promote progression.

I think Kings, Queens and conquerors got this wrong. Instead of taking over countries and destroying them. Rulers and governments should be sharing should have shared knowledge around the world; trading knowledge from country to country almost as a currency; promoting progress in the human species. In that approach the lengths the human species could accomplish is crazy. Furthermore if the aim is to become more powerful, then making the place where you conquer more powerful is advantageous to everyone.

"Well you can't be upset if you don't vote"

Once, when I was asked if I voted, I laughed... I laughed at the fact I know that "every vote counts". I just don't see any policy that is trying to help me. Usually after the ear ache of hearing how if the vote lands on someone you really don't want, then life would be terrible, I agree. However the political options are not good either way. I then would pose a thought I have on this topic which is "I will vote when someone represents me and everybody of sane mind". Why should I agree to choose the lesser of two evils? Two evils that have been given power by "us"? *And I'm ridiculous.* Maybe a stupid opinion to some; however either way we're F*%&$d. I will vote when there is a candidate who is representative of equal opportunities for socio-economically deprived communities. The thing is, I understand governments have to cater to their majority, which we sadly are not. However this isn't to say we cannot have power, or that someone from our minority cannot rule and represent the majority as well as ours and other minorities.

Every day in our lives we unknowingly walk through different systems of power and control. Power is a weird thing; a lot of people do not like to talk about power or who is really in control. Is power really with the people or majority? I have learnt that power is not good nor is power evil, power is as fundamental as an element of the periodic table. Eric Liu says power determines who determines the rules of the game (read that again if you must).

Power by definition is the ability to have others do, as you would have them do. Power is in all scenarios of life. There are six sources of power; force or violence, wealth, government, social norms, ideas and the majority. Force is the use of strength and violence as a means to exert power. This is usually the furthest length of power, seen in governments and empires throughout time. A small glimpse is the London riots, where a violent backlash was a demonstration of social discontent. The riots were a reaction to several proceedings, which demonstrated the power held by this group of people. Ways to obtain more power is using these six types of power and merging them to create more power.

Generating ideas and moving social norms can give power to a community. By changing your social norms to a higher level, you automatically give the next generation power. For example if the majority of my friends went into business or education, then in three years there would be that many more people who can influence and inspire our youth. We are in the start phase of our birth of power.

There are three laws of power. Firstly, power is never static. It is either growing or decaying. So in theory, if we are sitting idle, then we are being acted upon. If we are not actively looking to progress, then we are probably being put upon by someone else. Secondly, power flows in all every sector of life; politicians and others in positions of power use laws and policies to guide and direct the flow of power to their desired ideology. Lastly, power forms compounds; different powers can be combined to create a larger power.

In the search for power, you have to firstly see who has power and understand why it is like that. Then find who wants to keep it like that. Study and search for power so we can have a positive effect on history. Almost like the industrial revolution. This could be the Digital Culture Revolution. Maybe it is that time to make our imprint on history. "Be the author of change". I'm trying to write power into my brothers and sisters in situations similar to mine. In any situation you must express yourself, organise your thoughts then organise yourself. Try organizing those around you; practise building consensus and practise conflict -- all amazing parts of building power.

Be a hero

You are a hero just by doing you the best you can. Every day you leave your domain and take on the same tasks as a hero. You depart then go through trials and crises to obtain a treasure or power. You could be in school and you are overcoming the trials of trigonometry, and through assistance and receiving a result you are now a hero. Joseph Campbell [xv] has written a book on how to be a hero. Joseph writes that the similarity between all mythical and modern day heroes is that usually, they are normal humans. Who in turn have to go through his or her own trials, such as the ones that every human crosses every day. Just by having a positive view and becoming educated, you are a hero imposing a change of power in your own life circumstances.

Chapter 4 One

I think therefore I am.

Looking into the words of philosophers and highly regarded academics, I began to realise there was a huge emphasis on the universe and how it affects us. Don't worry… I'm not going to go all sci-fi, however they do make a lot of discoveries. The principle is basically asking the question "and what's that made of?!" several times over until you are stuck. We must all follow the same pattern; we are made of tiny things, which then are made of even tinier things and the list should go on forever theoretically or until you get to superstring theory, but that's for another book. We know that a tiny flu virus, so small you cannot see it, touches your skin or makes contact with you. It has affected the tiniest bacteria in your body and now you are sneezing. Alternately, we also know that if we eat well and exercise we can try and prevent ailments.

It's the exact same principle, treat the smaller bits correctly and the rest shall follow.

Now let's look at that idea more broadly: if you educate your children and peers about power and understanding, which are the universal generic ideas we should start from, then we have a chance to in a sense "eat well and exercise" by spreading ideas that will help and affect us in the long run.

Many theories from Da Vinci and Plato support the idea that life, ranging from the smallest atom to the far planets, all follows the same natural pattern as each other or some variation of it. This was named in ancient texts as the fruit of life. Essentially, it is the idea that the universe itself is an organism and we are all a part of its being. Look at it like this, inside your body your have millions of bacteria that are foreign to the human form. In fact studies show that people have bacteria not yet discovered by scientists residing in their gut. We know within our body we have bacteria constantly interacting with our own body, making us what we are today. Imagine this same concept however viewing human beings as the bacteria. This does agree with the theory that the universe is alive and we are a part of it, significant the role, or not. Could this be what human's mistake for god? This universal life we all partake in? Is the meaning of life humorously simple as just: "Live it"?

In order for a community to elevate itself, it is very simple. The individuals within the community have to want to excel. Imagine if everybody that lived on your road just became CEO's of all of the biggest corporations in the world. You could imagine the instant changes of your road's aesthetics... a couple golden Ferraris, big parties, maybe a jet or two. The environment changes as we change. This is a way we humans may have a natural effect on our surroundings rather than the other way round. If we push for self-improvement, then eventually our environment will follow.

"I aint saying I don't want to make money
But I'm tryna do the right things with it
If I eat food, eat food with my crew
See me and Dev in a cinema near you
And when I pull up to the premiere
Don't ask why I aint wearing a suit" - Skepta [xvi]

To see a change for our children and their children, we need to invest in ourselves. Invest into making yourself the best person you can possibly be. You can resource and build by helping those around you and building solid networks interlinking various parts of your social groups. Almost like the formula to success is actually based on teamwork.

Think of a business as a large human body with the head of the company being the directors or CEOs controlling the actual strategic straight-line movements. Then consider the heart to be the customer understanding and marketing and the hands and fingers are the workmen. I digress, countries follow the same trait, the head of the country being the government and monarchy, then the various vast roles that make a country or city work... this includes even the dustbin man. The better any of these bodies are treated the better it works within the world. Therefore in my opinion the first step to grasping this understanding of how life is a pattern that is imprinted on you starts with self-improvement of the mind, body and consciousness of your surroundings. I mean, exercise more, eat healthy, think calm and stress releasing thoughts. Essentially get rid of your bad energies by gaining control of your mind and everything will fall into place. Expand your view on the world and how you fit in it. Understand you have a large part to play in the world by just living and being yourself.

Humans are made of cells; in turn the cells are made of particles, which are then made of atoms, which are then made of protons, which are made of quarks the list goes on. However with this in mind, once you remove a proton or alter one of the latter then it will have an effect on the original cell. If we treat ourselves and our peers right, stay healthy and educate ourselves, we can better the place where our children shall live. Imagine the amazing heights human beings could then reach. Potentially end world hunger, or world poverty. They could run uncorrupt governments and an understanding policing system; the possibilities are endless. However it is our duty to mankind to do our best to raise the game and lift the invisible barriers for our children, and their children's children.

Life feeds us false facades and lies so we don't look deep into the importance of knowledge and progression mentally. We just focus on wealth. However even Russell Simmons[xvii] was recorded explaining how meditation is the way he became rich, I'm not telling everybody to start crossing their legs in the trap house and chant, but I am trying to tell my people specifically to be more mindful and understand that everything you say and do has an effect, so we need to educate not destroy.

After researching into religions and their origins, it's widely known that there was a time on earth that we broadly refer to as ancient times. Times prior to the pyramids and other ancient cultures, etc. where their studies match our modern day principles to make a solid business structure, family structure, friendship structure. It is clear you need strong foundations and support with a lot of careful planning because with our information helping those at the bottom we can never rise as a group. However I interpreted this as just 'do you the best you can". I understand the potential confusion; I am essentially telling everybody to be less selfish and work cohesively to make a smarter healthier version of yourself and in doing this you raise the status quo. Raise the social norms; spark the flame for progression.

Chapter 5   The underdog

"Fell in love with the game and it never loved me back,
all it ever did was turn me to a villain." -Yxng Bxne [xviii]

Let's be honest we are not made underdogs because of some divine plan to keep the divide. However, keeping the divide aligns well with an agenda of power. The whole point of power is to not let it go and to stay in power. Our social and economic position is just collateral in the overall war of power.

So it makes perfect sense for existing large corporations and government institutions to do everything they can to stay in power.

The economic differences in our societies are caused by the failings of modern day capitalism. Originally capitalism was created to supply society, where capitalism is accepted, with what it needed. Created only to self-serve, to find faults with our institutes and fix them with useful products, or skills or academics. However the push to always have more than our peers has distorted the original use of capitalism. Thus making it what we see today. By paying the workers less and decreasing the materials cost, we see wealthy CEO's and underpaid labourers. This can have unthinkable effects on the human condition. Diminishing the skills provided by labourers by paying them a small percentage of the money made from their hard work. You can see where this would affect the worker. Literally it puts a cap on their hard work.

Now we have a community of people who feel demoralised. A community of people, who have been beaten to submission, with a social understanding of "people like us don't..." However, some may argue that the idea of a meritocracy gives people, who are from deprived socio-economic circumstances, a chance to excel and become leaders. This was the idea of Napoleon 250 years ago, when he announced the reign of power and elite should not be blood based, yet based on the merits of intelligence. Therefore the idea that there is an unbridgeable gap is inconceivable to those on the other side of the bridge. However I argue that meritocracy is the biggest divide in capitalism, not because those who are deemed smart excel, but because those who are at the lower end of the meritocracy scale are deemed as failures and unfortunate. 250 years ago this would make perfect sense since that the socio economic divide was as normal as the sunlight or the moon. It was just there, people lived in societies where they understood the divide; luxuries were meant for kings and aristocrats whereas the common man was just a cog in the wheels of a machine. Yet meritocracy was not put in place for the common man, I argue meritocracy was put in place to rid the elite of incompetency, but not necessarily draft people from lower standards of living to govern.

Meritocracy gives birth to demoralisation because it sends out the subtle idea that those who succeed have merited their hard work and intelligence and those who don't are failures. How could this be true when there is such an imbalance within the educational system? Over 70 per cent of our government went to Russell group universities. *The Telegraph* released an article where they state that those who have private schooling are twice as likely to get into these universities. What does this tell us? How can our intelligence merit our success when education is not fairly distributed? Simply by keeping an educational divide, keeps the rich, rich. By saying the successful are responsible for their success due to their intelligence. You would also have to point out the unfortunates who are deemed unsuccessful are solely responsible for their lack of success, due to lack of intelligence.

"The underdog psychosis" is the result of subconsciously understanding the effects of meritocracy and capitalism. Moreover, what is the result on the young male or woman who is affected by underdog psychosis? There are usually two outcomes, sink or swim. To sink is the acceptance of socio-economic circumstances and not trying to make a positive change. On the other hand, to swim is the constant strive to change their circumstances. I mentioned earlier that those who are affected from "swim" underdog psychosis usually try to change their circumstances in vain. I say in vain because without a bespoke educational system, or guidance all too many of us usually turn to quick fixes such as crime.

"Swim" underdog psychosis is the lovechild of the socio-economically disadvantaged society and westernised capitalism. The idea that with enough hard work we will eventually get to the top, of our individual social and economic hierarchies, is ridiculous. We shouldn't try excelling in institutions that do not want us to excel. We need change. Instead, with the risk of being repetitive, we need to build and start our own institutions and foundations. Instead of following the diabolic path set for us.

Some may argue there are other individual reasons for the difference in the "sink" or "swim" underdog psychosis. Yet I believe there isn't one specific reason as to why a person is either one or the other it is actually just a result of all environmental attributes that make his/her personality.

To really define underdog psychosis we need to first understand the construction of society as it is today. We are told to live calmly and to strive for a job that is stable rather than a life-changing career because of the hurdles some of us are sure to come up against. We are a result of the fear our parents had for us. Some would say that our parents fear is to be expected, resulting in success being limited and defined as just economic stability. However I feel the beginning of the effects of underdog psychosis becomes apparent in the individual when a child moves from primary school in London to secondary school in London. We are very vulnerable to social change at this point. Surveys taken in secondary schools prove that children who live in socio-economically deprived (SED) conditions take more independence then their privately tutored peers. Children from SED communities usually journey home from primary school independently from a younger age; whereas children with more privileged backgrounds are brought home from school by parents and guardians until they start at secondary school.

Maybe the problem lies in not letting our children stay children long enough. But this can't be the sole problem; we don't want to be constantly between extremes trying to find a norm. We don't want to keep our children away from danger too much -- because we want them to build their character and prepare for lessons life will surely have to teach them. On the other hand, letting our vulnerable children have consistent contact with the corruption of youth that can be encountered living in cities like London, we do end up with the extreme that we find today. Instead we need to make the average person, our children encounter, be a Hero. We would have to create a society where the average mind-set is to promote forward thinking and progress for all on an equal basis

What we need is a society where the adults and older children, that our new generations encounter, have conscious mind-sets.

Chapter 6   The Psychosis

Westernised capitalism, the failings of a meritocracy and current
educational institutions, each in turn convince people of SED
circumstances that we are responsible for our own situation. Therefore
at the bottom of the food chain, instead of us assuming the best,
encouraging our youth and starting supportive institutions, we tend not
to guide our children or educate them on the hand that is against them.
With a lack of positive role models who engage with the youth, we are
instead left with those found in every society: the poor influences.

Underdog psychosis is a feeling that can come and go similar to the
feelings of love or hate. Underdog psychosis is a depression caused by
socio-economically deprived environments. Skepta's story about his
educational journey could have been told by any of my friends, and
could almost be applicable to all of them.

He speaks about misbehaving in school due to the lack of stimulation in education. Here we see the effect of the early schooling system within communities in socio-economically deprived areas, where with such a poor student to teacher ratios and other daunting factors, students fail to receive the attention they need. He then says that "school was not very hard", he just did not apply himself because in his mind he had already convinced himself that he would never become the person he thought he could aspire to become. The public schooling system has a trait that doesn't cater to all the children who attend the school. In most cases, rather than understanding why the student is being disruptive, the modern teacher would remove the disruptive child so as to not disturb the other children's learning; although effective and somewhat beneficial to the majority, no one takes time to address why Tyrone is being disruptive.

After this loss of stimulation in learning we look to stimulate ourselves elsewhere. Like Skepta, many of my peers and I smoked weed... this probably also made us subconsciously conform to what society expected us to do... but hey ho. The way drugs are introduced is interesting, because what's depression without a little bit of drug use. So what do you expect a person who feels like a black sheep and can easily obtain weed, to do? This is when a person who is going through depression finds something that separates them from reality; thus beginning the culture we have today. Imagine, you're arriving at school fully charged, and not in any suitable state to learn. Instead you're just constantly thinking I am never going to pass... should I even bother going to class? Fuck that. Responses fuelled by the communal understanding that there's no point trying because you cannot win.

What is the black sheep effect? It is feeling alone in a classroom of your kids meant to be your peers. It is knowing that you're likely to fail because everyone you know has. It is combined with your lack of self-confidence because, to be honest, you know you're not as smart as them and they fucking failed so you're doomed mate. This is the black sheep effect, the feeling of difference and the feeling of being alone with nobody who understands. Every stage of this development all has a small part to play in the overall feeling of underdog psychosis.

Finally I can answer what underdog psychosis is.

Underdog psychosis is a type of depression caused by two environmental factors.

Firstly, the effects of deprived socio-economic circumstances are:

I)   If the person has a low socio-economic status, then others who view the world as a meritocracy may look down on them, thus letting society have lower expectations for them.

II)   With lower expectations people tend to adhere to their expectations. This is commonly known as a "self-fulfilling prophecy"

III)   Parents and communities are less likely to be able to cater entirely for every need their youth may have.

IV)   People from higher social classes treat those from their inferior class as if they do not disserve to be treated equally, which has an accumulative adverse effect.

Secondly, the input received from their environment, including the media and education, where:

I)   There is a universal lack of positive role models in our media that show renowned people or insightful individuals from humble beginnings, people that kids raised in socio-economically challenged communities could aspire to follow.

II)   The media depicts the current stereotypes which young susceptible mind-sets may take to be reality and try to emulate.

III)   News outlets and places where information is given to the public can sometimes demonise individual cultures and communities by only producing negatively themed stories that the person watching may internalise. Even more so when you are immediately labeled as a hoodie, the media helps belittle some cultures.

IV)   The message that SED communities send their youth may be that the most they should aspire to life as a hustler, instead of giving their child a predisposition that they should aspire to something that provides them with a stable life.

V)   Educational curriculums barely show the presence of equal power in any subject, from the history that is taught to the literature that is read.

VI)   Some teachers are affected by their own class-ridden disposition, which in turn can have a negative effect on an individual's learning.

Chapter 7   The End

Every motion, every thought, every sound, everything; it all affects you. But understand that you are being influenced; it is up to you to choose what influences you. Life is hard; it is full of ups and downs. We are humbled and pray for stability when we are down and take leaps for success when we are up. We learn lessons through our mistakes, but our environment also teaches us. My message is that it is up to us to learn the right things from our environment.

We are in an age where information can travel around the world in seconds, all accessible from a mobile phone. Old techniques of power are being modernised and refined, leaving us with a politically correct corrupted state. The largest corporations, who have the time and money to invest into their own corporate and personal progression, run the largest countries. Even if that progression means that only an elite will run this country. Obviously from an aristocratic point of view; where's the issue? But from an underdog point of view we can obviously see the failings. The poor social care, the poor wealth distribution, the poor education system that doesn't teach you how to survive as an independent adult in the city you are raised and many more shortcomings that I haven't mentioned. The power structure is terrible at this current stage therefore we need to be proactive to obtain equal power for ourselves; educating our youth and teaching them that we all are equal and we can all obtain knowledge, this is power. Hopefully in the future, one of our kids will run for prime minister and incite a change. It starts with us; nurturing the next generation to greatness, whilst becoming great role models ourselves we can most likely make the path more real.

Our culture is one of the only cultures that the mainstream industries are trying to tap into. The large industries tend to sell to the majority... and the majority aren't rich. Therefore if you want to sell something in bulk, then it should be aimed towards the middle and lower classes. Yes, we are the majority, and yes we are buying back our own culture from people who had no hand in making it. Culture is made up of traditions or beliefs of a group of people. We have built a culture from our misfortune. Two things make a culture; the presence of customs and cultural forms of expression. A custom is a frequently repeated act that is a characteristic of the culture of the people performing the act. Cultural forms of expression are the essence of a culture, such as the music, the fashion and the food. Although rising out of an act of depression, lack of self-confidence is what keeps our culture dwelling in the lanes of crime and lack of progression.

However we should take pride in the fact that our culture is our foundation. We should be confident knowing that on this culture, we can build our own institutions. It is ours and we have the power to influence a large number of people because they feel the same as we do.

Society, as we know it today, stems from the reactions and actions of our predecessors, or in some cases the lack of action. Apart from the information we gain through education, our environment also teaches us. Yet this urge to learn more has really been the foundation for our own demise. Taking a glance at history, it is clear certain individuals have had the power and ability to obtain knowledge; **but it is** their opinions and ideologies that have shaped the viewpoints of the underdog. Yet in doing so, they have left out the fact that if you want to appeal to the majority, your first port of call should be appealing to the underdogs themselves.

For new institutions and corporations to flourish and for established institutions and brands to diversify they need to merge and work cohesively with each other. Therefore the idea that people want to "abolish" large corporations altogether is crazy, these large corporations that we despise have the time and money at their disposal to diversify and expand our market.

Why do you think large clothing companies love to give free clothes to all of the larger UK rap/grime artists. Not only because they are at the forefront of our culture but also because we are a new demographic, a young culture that doesn't own established fashion institutions that support its own scene, and they know we are a large group of consumers who do not consume from each other. However we can be self-sustaining and self-sufficient; we have already made steps to control our media, through the likes of GRM Daily, Link up TV and SBTV. We need to slowly start building our cultural institutions and not let our voice be left out of history.

My daughter was born on the 19th of January 2016, I want to know she can grow to be anything she wants to be; not feeling the glass ceiling our parents feel and/or have felt. I want her not to feel that a lifestyle revolved around crime should **not** be idolised. Hopefully she will be able to watch some diverse cartoons, or when she gets older, watch movies about black people that do not show them in a bad light or as a sidekick, unless historically relevant. A diverse market is a flourishing market with new competition and new consumers.

My point is that positive change is a progressive change for everyone;

we can empower societies and change the dynamics of the London and other western markets, whether it is fashion, media, art or business as a whole.

Distribution of wealth has historically been imbalanced. However, the way we treat the socio-economically deprived groups doesn't make sense for progression. We need to invest time into building new institutions and schemes, which in the long run will expand our current markets to take heed of the needs of everyone, rather than a select few.

Finally, the idea of the underdog is derived from Greek tragedies and myths that portray the simple message that the worst things happen to normal everyday people. It is our job to continue to live and learn from the heartaches we experience and to try to understand more through our mistakes. We can learn a lot from tragedies; they teach us that life is universal and without action we are being acted upon. Life can be tragic at times. So for underdogs that feel alone and singled out, just remember life is routing for you.

Let's always remember that like Youngs Teflon we can switch roles in life.

"When we used to kick ball
We always put him in goal
Just a little tale
How a boy can switch roles

Used to send to the shop

Kept things at his mums

Guess he just wanted a little homage from his dons

Always the nigga at the back

Just a baby fam

Used to stay out late so he could roll with the pack

But the mind is a terrible thing to waste

Through time you can see him trying change

Money is the route to all evil

And power bring the worst of people

Watch how you treat the feeble

Used to be a worker now he run his own line

Starting team he ain't off the goal line

And his memory was tight

Even though he's getting it now

He still don't forget all the old times

Swear we always put him in goal

Just a little tale how a boy can switch roles" - Youngs Teflon[xix]

ENDNOTES

[i] Skepta, Song title?, *Title of Album?*, Release date?

[ii] The quote: *"The cave you fear to enter holds the treasure you seek"* is ascribed to Joseph Campbell.

[iii] Skepta- Mastermind

[iv] Willie Lynch quote: Letter 1712

[v] Skepta, 'Castles' *Blacklisted*, 2012

[vi] Quote attributed to Sigmund Freud in a conversation, 1897

[vii] Devlin featuring Skepta, '50 Grand', single, 2015

[viii] Georg Wilhelm Friedrich Hegel German philosopher, 1770-1831

[ix] Selim Bassoul quote: source?

[x] Quote source?

[xi] Descartes, 1644

[xii] Yxng Bane, Doubted Me, 2016

[xiii] Plato, Greek philosopher, ca. 428 – ca. 437 BCE

[xiv] Eric Liu, *TED talk*, 2014.

[xv] Joseph Campbell, *Hero With a Thousand Faces*, 1949/ 1972, Princeton: Princeton University Press

[xvi] Skepta, Blacklisted

[xvii] Russell Simmons, Insert a Net address?

[xviii] Yxng Bxne, 'Villain', *Full Moon*, 2016

[xix] Youngs Teflon, Young Bull, *January sales*, 2016

Printed in Great Britain
by Amazon